COLLECTEI

30. 06.

28.

20. 10. 97

1h 98

12. 06. 98

RAFFERTY, Sean

Collected poems

40002272| £12.95

Please return/renew this item by the last date shown
Thank you for using your local library

By the same author

16 Poems (Grosseteste Press, 1973)
Poems 1940-1982 (privately printed, 1990)
Peacocks. Full Stop (Poetical Histories, 1993)
Salathiel's Song (Babel, 1994)

Seán Rafferty

COLLECTED POEMS

Edited by Nicholas Johnson

CARCANET

First published in 1995 by
Carcanet Press Limited
402-406 Corn Exchange Buildings
Manchester M4 3BY

A CIP catalogue record for this book
is available from the British Library
ISBN 1 85754 124 3

The publisher acknowledges financial assistance
from the Arts Council of England

Set in 10 pt Times by Bryan Williamson, Frome
Printed and bound in England by SRP Ltd, Exeter

Funded by
THE
ARTS
COUNCIL
OF ENGLAND

For Christian

A Note

I would like to thank Clare and Michael Morpurgo, Ted and Carol Hughes, and Nicholas and Kate Johnson for their help over the years. I would also like to thank Kevin Perryman and Peter Riley for publishing a book and a pamphlet for me.

S.R.

Acknowledgements

Some of these poems were first published by *Odysseus* (USA, 1972), *Grosseteste Review* (1972), *PN Review* (1982), *Peacocks was really great* (1992), *Babel* VII (1993) and *Peacocks Two* (1993).

Contents

V

VI

VII

VIII

IX

I

The bubbles rise in the glass.
When I was young
I thought there could be no end
of the songs to be sung.
Now I grow old
with one tune flat in my head
to be up and out and away:
alive or dead.

Over the bright the bare
bright spring bare winter day
moved every living thing
to rivalry and play
I saw three hawks go up
and bear the crown away.

Carry the crown from sight.

Under that emptied sky
dwarfed desirous blind
man has a mind to fly.
In that spiral caught
earth air dominion's king
must feather thought on thought
to join creation's ring.

That empyrean game
Kings and their kestrels play.
Your eyas' wings were tame
your feet grew cold on clay
your robe was all to rags
your crown of buckled straws
a scarecrow in a field
fouled by crows and daws.

It was the tale she loved to tell:
half child she wakened half afraid
foundling among the flowers, their fall
to change a cradle made her bed.
On that green bank she leaned her head.
An air of birds above the wood
the cloud pack haring on the hill.
But when she rose Creation stood
in a confederate wonder. Still.

A pretty tale to give a boy
come tumbling out of plenty's horn
and heir to orchards. What had I?
A share in sand: under the thorn
I pitch and lie where I was born.
And nothing left for man to know
I follow from so fair a start?
I am my mother's son. I show
the blooded hand, the murderous heart.

Since I am man
and caught in sin
why then should I complain
my sentence is unjust?
And yet I must
although by doing so I sin again.

And yet I do.
And since you know
the long arrears I owe
You: is there no way
that I can quit and pay;
Punish me Lord but do not plague me so.

Let envy burn
me; let me toss and turn
sleepless in sloth, be torn
torn between angers, dosed with my own lust
at least my pride could boast
commensurate pain. But take away this thorn.

This thorn. I mean
this pointless pin
prick under my skin
crept body buried there.
Lodge it elsewhere.
Find it another flesh to foster in

festers in me.
Could it not be
Your instrument elsewhere, healing, remedy.
Is there no bore
a thorn might cure
by daily needling, homeopathy.

Or is there here
for me some share
of your mysterious working whereby I
have from no peace these nine months penned no line
now intertwine
a sort of poem and a kind of prayer.

For Nicholas Johnson

Where the breached wall begins the traveller sees
clumped thistles standing and the roots of trees
antlered above the park's tall summer grass.
But has a mile to go before he'll pass
the ruin of a lodge where one stone post
stands for the gates, the avenue is lost
and laurelled over. A great house is gone
he'll say, he's meant to say, and hurry on
under the sombre fir trees, not to guess
the luxury tended in this wilderness.

But, say, he had time to turn aside and crawl
and waste and clamber, the good luck to fall
only in shallow bogs; say some mishap,
better not call it luck, some ragged gap
framed a full view in thorns; he'd see it all
in just the time it takes a boy to pull,
birdnesting time, the churchyard boughs apart
and look at nothing in the yew's dry heart.
At nothing. There it stands: but now so near
and come so far and, look, the way is clear
only this length, once lawn, of waving grass.
Trees draw their darkness up to let him pass
terraces rise to meet him, the great doors
open, and rooms receive; the marble floors
or stone, oak, echo; and the double stair
like some upended wishbone and as bare
leads to bare rooms above; an emptiness
which will not furnish not the smallest guess
who built or owned this house and who will come
today as yesterday to one small room
will come tomorrow, like a thief must come
back stairs odd hours to one small airless room
to that small airless attic where a ghost
signs the dead name across a mirror's dust.

The old stag crew before the light
and there and near it sang amends
for dwindled ash and candle ends
and for the page that looked as though
a bird had grounded on the white
the pure impediment of snow.

The ash and ends the draughts that mouse
over the floor, the adding clock,
tick and half tick, owl's chimney talk,
rats' honeymoons, I thought I knew
the hour's small noises through the house:
and suddenly the old stag crew.

What early light had edged his comb?
He clapped his wings and made time fly
like dust from feathers and his cry
went raftering back till it was heard
beyond the straw built rooves of Rome;
o dawn bright sill o gilded bird.

Aristodemus wakened up
cradled in a cramp, a mouth like plush,
eyes stuck in glue and tried to push
the night away and belched and through
the rift he made he saw the cup
and it was then the old stag crew.

A far cry on a favouring wind:
the great cup passed from left to right:
what star have I outwatched tonight
I sit no longer time's dull child.
But I have sat to supper's end
and heard the muses reconciled.

The more the rocketry goes up
the more my eyes look down;
for all the Buzz above my head
I'll walk a wary man.
A barefoot boy in summer grass
I trod on carrion.

He counted up his ha'pence
the golden silence broke;
He said I was an acorn once
I might have been an oak;
the first to go are livelier
than those who last too long.
I lived to be a proverb
I might have died a song.

II

Many a man that sang of love
as though his love stands there
or lies unlatched and listens
for his footstep on the stair.
But sat beside a dying fire
unwilling and afraid
that he might climb to find a ghost
cold in his sheeted bed.

In May the month of miracle
flower on the black bough
flower on the green leaf;
in May the flower the frost the fall
the month of May is all my grief.

The white hawthorn the lilac massed
to dwarf my mourning where I passed;
they were like alien angels come
before their time to greet her home.

Too early come the cruel frost
that claimed my love too early lost
their promise for a tribute gave
and wept their flowers into her grave.

In May the month of miracle
flower on the black bough
flower on the green leaf;
in May the flower the frost the fall
the month of May is all my grief.

It was a folly of my grief
that broke the branch and set it there
in heavy splendour, flower and leaf
bowed to the midnight air.
And still no footstep on the stair.
I thought that if a ghost should come
the scent of flowers will guide her home.

Last spring from that same tree she brought
the smouldering lilac wet with rain
and set it where it stands, the thought
is all my thought; and pain.
She brought and will not bring again.
And for that thought and pain I kept
the tears my childhood never wept.

How short a time since war and death
mourned at our marriage. She is dead.
Go stumble in the streets beneath
the flags that will not lift your head
into their peace and hush unsaid
under the cheering crowds your cry
that they should live and she should die.

The nights you walk my love my sleep
I waken from the dream
into that dreadful ward of death
where you must die again.

Am I the culprit ghost whose feet
steal on forbidden ground?
I would not have it so or sleep
unless the dead sleep sound.

How could I know you now my love
from any other one
or you know me, for life can do
more things than death has done.

But come tonight before I sleep
I shall not speak or cry
but we shall take as midnight strikes
a formal, strange, goodbye.

This moment where I fill the glass
holds neither life nor death
but we shall drink so I have read
the wine and the wine's breath:

and in that fragrance heard and seen
surrounds us at the end
streets squares and gardens where we walked
and every flower and friend.

        May absence be as kind and clear
        as midnight air between
        the moon and the moon's image
        in the still stream.

How long was this ago? Under what sign
the Bull, the Ram was such a wonder seen?
Did Alexander or some Pharaoh reign
or before that, how long before, how long?

It was that spring the blackbird learnt its song.

Come down to earth: the golden toys are lost
the amber ornaments, there lie at least
traces of ash down in the dug for dust
will date the summer when this phoenix flamed.

It was that summer when the flowers were named.

But when such wonders walk, the earth and air
rumour her progress through the marvellous year;
signs follow portents barren fruit trees bear
fresh springs will flow and did no comet shine?

This was the autumn of the elm and vine.

And now what harvest, barn and cask and hive
feeds the fourth season when dark nights are long
and cold? What sustenance survives:
                                        survive
midnight and meditation memory song

Look to no living face
in hope to find
your longing for that lost
her promise of that place;
far other domicil
all lovers claim at last:
the hollow in the hill
where two may lie and rest.

III

I saw her sleeping. See her, saints, tonight
across the undreamed of darkness safe to light.
Make her no changeling in the changing night.

Pleasure and summer's child
orphan while still unborn
far into sorrow exiled.
And exiled in a land
where hooded with their woe
the solitary mourn.
In grief's prevailing wind
the winter earth, the thorn.

So once among the shades
the stolen child was Queen;
suffer the heavy crown
but keep your garland green.
Quick to the impulse give
the freedom of your blood
cage in your heart the dove.
And in your speech the note
of all the birds who sang
with that most summer sun
like honey in the throat.

Now by your head I place
in lieu of angels these
ancestral images
of dusk and peace and night:
the wild geese when they trace
over the Solway sky
an alphabet of flight;
a cloudless crescent moon
still waters mirror deep
with one companion cloud;
moon, moon and swan, asleep.

Heart be the flowering branch
to house a singing bird
that all who pause may swear
a flower in song they heard.

Heart never still yet have
no motion of your own;
dance the descended guest
tremble when he is gone.

On the green hill of childhood keep
your festival; untroubled sleep
and laughing wake beside the earlier sun
that over one hill and five fields has come,
so near is heaven still, to be
your consort this and each unclouded day.
And by such a marriage, look, your home
first to a kingdom then a world is grown
and more than these a garden; now and far
the meadows and the fallow fields prepare
a progress, flower by flower, and war in this
but in all else, o happy Queen, at peace.
So climates continents will crowd to be
blessed in your sphere; northward you will see
dawn alps of apple April; southward go
few furlong months till high above you sway
the bracken's green and fronded Africa.
But shun the discovered West. Eastward there is
a more than Asia. Eastward Eden lies
and you are home, your home. Run where you will
you cannot trespass, if you fall you fall
only where grass is soft; though ripe fruits reach
into your mouth they do not tempt but teach
a simple lesson and no sin to eat:
the sloe how bitter but the bramble sweet.

You grow like a beanstalk
as tall as a tale;
twining your time a garland, the leaves are all
shaped in a single heart, to climb until
you stand as high as your wish and what's over the wall
flowers in your eye, a marvel, to teach the tongue
the scale of tomorrow and elsewhere. The song to be sung.

Once, o legends ago,
in the halfway house
by the fire where bedward candles beg their flame
I read you the tale of the thumb-tall girl who was swept
away on a lily leaf, the toad, the mouse;
you so still on my lap I thought you slept.
But the story darkened. The mole's long galleries came
nowhere to guess or glimmer of ending; grief.
Tears that would not, would not be comforted, no
though the risen bird was king and south was home
would not: away on a woman's tears far past belief
in a happy ever and after I watched you go
Ceres in search of her child a child gone down to the dark.
I heard you a woman cry
and born a maiden you wept for the maidens who die.

Soon I listen
and you, the traveller, make
plans for an early start; your turn to tell
the other side of the story. The path you take
is worn like a wish: beasts are clumsy and kind
the birds are concerned about orphans, nothing has changed, the lake
copies its only landscape of turrets and trees, you find
the house they told you was ruined and there at last
the sun is taking the girl in her bridal dress,
the six white horses are waiting, across the park
bells are rising, immaculate doves fly past
over your future and after them into the dark
my fears go up like fireworks, salute and bless
as far as a wish can see or a heart can guess.

A girl before her glass
intent as women are
on lips and cheek and hair
she cannot know;
what company she has
how many dark and fair
surround her come and go
deliberate and pass:

and her own mother there.

IV

William Woolsery is dead
down in shillet dig his bed;
toll the three score years and ten
toll the bell ten times again.

William Woolsery is no more
he had three wives and nearly four
ask the fourth and she will tell
five foot Willie loved me well.

William Woolsery's passed away
pheasants dance and partridge play
hares grow merry and by night
leap the long furrows in delight.

Fade you now for ever airs
Willie jigged at country fairs
fade by fading bar room fires
scandals of forgotten squires.

Count no more on Saturday
won at home or lost away
lost to home and far abroad
William goes to meet his God.

An old man mumbling in a public bar
of that long wintered storm of war
drove him abroad, is beaten by the names
of villages his battles battered down.
He loots a desert, lets a river drown,
it was you would believe to hear him tell
Geography gone up in smoke and flames
the biggest shambles known this side of Hell.

'Barbarous, master, barbarous; naught went right
the heat could maze you mad you lay at night
rumped up like turds and shivered; agues, mules,
vipers; as long as, longer: thieves with knives
stab you as soon as look they would, their wives
were dirty and wore gold. I've travelled, sir.'
The story he could tell them ignorant fools;
dysentery, cognac, clap; wound, ribbon, star.

Nobody left to contradict or care
what war before which war he fought or where
or why: and yet the helmet home
and the worn coin, worth something, that's no lie;
the wound that he can tell the weather by
make written history a fumbled braille
for unbelievers. War's true idiom
in this untrue interminable tale.

Hark on him now. 'I told you on't before
a master windy place, there was a tower
we set afire: but what I'd tell about
is the tall captain I was groom for then;
what was his name, a proper gentleman
but on in age when I was but a boy;
king's cousin, some said, brave: but dead I doubt.'

Could he be Agamemnon. Was it Troy.

Old men and their mythologies. I speak now
of Alfred Woodroll once was my one customer
many a winter's morning. I knew his step well.
Cut away coat and breeches Alf stood by the bar

and talked. His talk was horses, 'osses, hunting men
field masters, whips, followers to hounds who met
by the crosses, on village squares, dented the tended lawns
of now forgotten houses; Alf did not forget

Miss Casement, Mrs Cap'n James, these side saddle ladies
no ditch nor five bars daunted as they sped
hard hatted over the October stubble the unwired hedges
'Where are they now?' I'd say. Said Alf, 'They're dead.'

Then off; away. Horseman and horse in one old cantering centaur
over the floor's five parishes, up with the pack,
'Tis bitches make the music'; checks by the table
kills somewhere near the fire comes hacking slowly back

to his half pint; no more. No more. Dismount and mourn.
I speak now of Alfred Woodroll. I praise his judging eye
and his cures and coping skills because I would not
have a remembering man only remembered by

a tarnished cap and the grinning mask of a death
or his name be forgotten among fields when a horn will sound
from the foxy brakes. I speak of him I speak too
of Flash the nimble roan; Samson the noble hound.

Rumour of winter in a running wind;
cold news at corners under creaking signs;
ill weather for an old wound.

Stagnant October soaked and spoiled; the lanes
rutted; stogged gateways; hedgerows rusted out;
the slop of autumn choking in the drains.

Now in the fruitless branches starlings sit
mocking the orchard, in a chequered flock
the plover lift like snow and fall like soot.

I saw the ghost of summer in the smoke
of blackened flowers were lately red and white;
I saw the saplings stripped by the brook.

Our days stand huddled in what's left of light;
small griefs sit round the heart and steal its warm;
and life kneels humbled at the chimney's foot.

The cold a trance, the dark a wicked charm
can turn a talent in its burial ground
till fingers ghost below the severed arm.

Rumour of winter in a running wind;
what's past is wasted, what's to come unkind;
here's ill weather for the old wound.

The night's as dark as a sack
road's turned into a field
field's run into a ditch
neither chick nor child

should be out on a night like this
and especially me can't fly
or bawl or scrawl dear God
what a way for a hero to die

with only three beers inside
unless you count the third:
dress by the right, Advance
Oh help fire mother mur-

der. Bees. I'm stung.
It's a hornet stinged my lip;
wasps this time of the year
the whole world's ass to tip.

Bigod it's a holly bush.
I know who planted it here.
The one that lost my cap
the same one pinched my beer

knowing my short cut home.
I wish he'd told me it first.
Will some genelman light me a star?
What a terrible thing's a thirst.

Think of the battles I won,
think of mother and kids
maybe you'd better not
will some genelman hand me the pledge?

Hand me the pledge. I'll sign
if you'll write it for me, I'm lame.
Feel me I'm all baptized.
Joy will be the name.

. . ./

The saints of the Lord kneeled down
but they never kneeled in a ditch.
Fall in my squad fall in.
Get up you son of a bitch.

But did I hear or dream of that old man
was parson of his parish fifty years;
eager to give, avid for men to have
Christ's crumb and comfort; diligent in prayer
against false doctrine, the indifference
of silent pews under six silent bells
dust in the font: God's dust. 'Thy will be done
for thine', but April's 'Kingdom glory', light
windowed its weather on the leaded pane,
mirror of meditation, glowed and dimmed
dazzled and dimmed and fetched him from his knees
into the sun to lean against a stone
among wind slanted stones: Farleys and Brookes
and Arnolds of this parish, Ansteys, Knights;
to read the dead the service for the dead,
dearly beloved and sadly missed and gone
before; now reunited and at rest
under the grass and weed the thickening fleece
of dandelion hides their humps and mounds;
to tell the dead the resurrection of the dead.
'For as in Adam, so in Christ', his voice
lost in a flap of jackdaws, on the path
a song thrush cracked a snail against a stone.
Out and above him in the temporal day
a tractor climbed a hill, two contrails crossed
and laddered down the sky. 'Behold I show;
and look no farther from me than a stone
roped down with ivy to its grave in grass
or the first drifting snow but now in Spring,
and every spring: Behold a miracle.
God's blood in Lebanon whose footstep here
in clay and shillet planted in the West
windflowered anemones? In that same wind
that waves the green length of the winter corn
along bare hedgerow's aerial ashpoles; wind
the dandelion seeds. I saw it flower
out of the wintry grave and from the grave,
fledged on a breath, His breath, the air I breathe,
vagula, nudula, I see the soul
the migrant soul uncertain of its way
circle till faith a true direction find
and fly, look Emperor, home.'

V

Woodlands winter
where leaves were green:
my red is the rowan
my white the gean.

I speak of a valley.
I call at morning
the roll of its farms
till cocks reply.
From the cobbled yards
they cry and eastwards
the first leaf stirs
in a hush of doves.

I speak of a river.
I herd the fleece bright
flock of its springs
till driven streams
are loud in the fold
I lead its waters
to praise among pastures
their hartstongue home.

I speak of a childhood.
I lay a nightlong
fable of sleep
till morning sang
in the green of the light
between leaf and language
a birth a ballad
a bird alone.

Ballad and childhood
and psalm and river
in the cup of my hands
I priest its praise;
I speak of a valley
and shall for ever
out of my numbered days.

The mower late in graveyard grass
sharpened his scythe to cut for me
green roads my barefoot summers pass
like Israel's children through the sea

a meadow's hay; where mowers lie
in hawthorn shade, to brim and bring
their pitcher from the conduit, I
the barefoot servant haycock king.

What is this road that I retrace
why should this water that I spill
rechristen me? He set my face
for home does home lie further still.
Some sabbath sung predestined place
Sharon Siloam under Sion's hill

Reteach I pray when I must pray
the passion of my childhood's prayer
that when day comes its knives will spare
the corncrakes nested in the hay.

Four acres of a northern farm:
their star marked inches claimed at last
over how many meadows passed;
not my loved meadow bring them harm.

To whom the clouds and winds were kind:
but fly and no man count your flight;
only at dusk his untold tale
tell you are gone to leave behind
a silence in the northern night
unbroken by the nightingale.

Because I have no son
that boy seems half my own
will leave his rod or gun
and let the pigeons fly;
waters in sunlight run
stilled under shadow lie.

Body and mind despise
the named the tamed the known
what touches, tendrils, ties
he's for the moors alone
to taste what no man tilled
drink at the source of streams
because his mind is filled
filled with heroic dreams.

He's where his dreams have found
close to the restless sky,
where else, a neutral ground
for clouds and dreams to race
their shadows in the sun
under the kestrel's eye.
But give his dreams the prize
what dreams his dreams have won;
laurel and choric song.

And when the sun climbs down
when he must turn to face
a night that falls too soon
the dark reverse alone:
give him a popular tune
to whistle down the long
dark long last loaning home.

Who walk this side of silence still?
long since to sleep a day's work done
across the fields over the hill
the harvesters are home and gone.
Who walk this side of silence still?

The harvesters are home and gone;
their meadows sleep till early light
the water sleeps beside the stone.
Who calls this late their last goodnight?
the harvesters are home and gone.

Who call this late their last goodnight?
their roads are dark, how far their bed?
Listen. Beyond our blindfold sight
are they the living we the dead.
Who call this late their last goodnight?

Too late, too late, for time to put
another feather in my bed.
Content. Content. I raise my hat
to ladies and the passing dead.

Late at e'en drinkin the wine
me mysel thegither
I have altercation with
the skeleton my brother.
Time's on his side.
He does it out of pride

'I have lugged the flesh along
like a guilty parcel
by the streams of Babylon
exile over I s'all;
Annan water wading deep
I shall lay me in a sleep
deeper than the Rochell.'

Rowan by the red rock, plead,
gean, white gean, in the green holm intercede
for him,
dipper in your flying vestments stay
midstream on the dripping stone to pray
for him
on the first morning of his final day.

VI

1945

'Where are they now,' said Jack. Ironfoot Jack, this is,
after the war, that was, hitched on a bomb site corner
of Greek Street; rolling a splendid tear
down that same sprigged satin waistcoat; where
and wherefor ancient mourner

wherefor now stopst thou me. For who they were I knew
but where they are who knows, if he would know,
where are the children of Cheap or the squires of Alsatia
and all whom fire whom war, the Law, and hunger overthrow.

Spielers shlemils after this last dispersal
layabouts grafters; where do the buskers chant
along the mournful gutters of everweeping Paddington
or in the south suburbs by the Elephant.

How shall they sing the same songs in a strange land remembering
the lamplit West the pennies rained like rain;
goodnight sweet baby heart's delight Vienna
old dreamsongcities. Night. Auf wiedersehen.

Return musicians; the loud voice is gone
the Aryan brag, return civilian muse.
No one will listen. Over this sick infirmary
black sister of desolation sing me the blues.

No one will listen. The streets are full of noises
hallalis halleluias sackbuts psalteries tim
brels trumpets artillery: He has chastened the righteous
and utterly flattened the wicked. Praise Him.

A mandolin plays in a demolished café bar
ouvert la nuit Wide to the starry skies;
two snowdrops stalk the sidewalks of Dean and Compton
gunning for niggers dreaming of apple pies.

...../

Magnus ab integro saeclorum nascitur ordo.
Peace on a visit is lodging at Brown's Hotel.
Her head has been shaved. Miracles happen daily.
A shower of lump sugar has fallen on Clerkenwell.

High over ruin and reason the tower from twice rocked foundations
shoulders faith like a firkin into the morning air;
out of a hole in a wall was the great hooped window
Saint Anne considers her parish; a heart laid bare.

Marshall Street baths and Peter Street school and Berwick market
and the Lock and the Lex and the summer house in the square;
the Madrid the Belgian bar Madame Maurer, that other lady,
sometimes the infidel spares whom God would spare.

Stay with us now, patronne, homeless among the homeless,
mère de Madame ta fille; poor, as we are, not proud:
you know it all you have known it all for ever
who sewed the boy child's vest who stitched the hanged man's shroud.

Who sat on a bench by your door of a spring evening
with your back to the Avenue traffic content to share
your yard with children and cats and drunks and couples;
erect, black shawled, a peasant; I have seen you there.

Stay with us now: with the dim on Credulity corner
with the poor, their bones and belongings under a sack
on a grating; with the sick the busy the wicked
the broke and the bent and the jokers; Jeannot Gianni Jack.

Jack. Professor Jack. Jack with a box. The peripatetic
with his portable fourth dimensional Freudian fruit machine;
Jack the promoter of cafés; coffee and chess for Marxists,
tea for waltzing transvestites. Can such things, then, have been?

They were: but not for long. In no time the Bow Street runners
arrived in sequins and plimsolls to close that ball.
Jack conducted his own defence, calling on Edward Carpenter
Havelock Ellis St John the beloved. They did him no good at all.

                                                    .../

Two years.

And now from a longer stretch a war worse than Wormwood
Jack has come back to his manor with its flaglit festive air
of a busted fairground to stand alone on a corner,
the timid voice of a stranger asking a stranger; where.

Where are the Ernies, the three of them, Big and Little and Dirty
and Sailor Ben and Jack, mad Jack, the other one
distilling Shivovitza to a recipe of Kropotkins;
and Pistol and Nym and Bardolph, what hinders them from home.

A man past middle age with an iron brace on his left leg
wearing an old frock coat and a frayed black stock
and a fancy waistcoat stands on a corner
of a street that calls itself Greek Street under a stopped clock.

It is roughly, peacetime, eleven on a sunny morning.
The old man says no more. He makes no play
with a stick or wand. All he does is to alter
the month and the year and the weather and the time of the day

to a dusk in early spring: the rained on empty pavements
surface like causeways, the lamps in a smoky haze
are yellow and furred like mimosa, the fruit on a late street barrow
in the light of a wineshop window: a mandolin plays

through the idling deepening dusk, in a Compton Street café bar,
a balalaika's song. Behind the web of lace
curtain the misted windows Time is recording
that spring, that year, this place.

1959

Never go back. I knew that. Never years after
not even in sunlight in winter in winter's sunlit cold
go back to such streets and remember on every corner
the young lived here and now; these young are dead or old.

So I went back: webfoot across the traffic
contrary against crowds I went back in the gloom
headbent in a drizzle of autumn and turned for comfort
into a bar was a bar was more like a tomb

or a tidy morgue with a licence now open for custom,
no matter how many, the size or the sex, could lie
stiffly out stretched on those pink formica tables
no ghost could unbend at that counter: no more could I.

So where? At this unbewitching hour when shops draw shutters
and kitchens stir under halflit restaurants
and the lounger tires of the ads in the evening papers
and the sons and daughters of music tire of recorded song.

But the long straight street in the thin rain.
Demolitions delapidations; scaffolding girders hoardings; landmarks
        shored
against these ruins. Bertorelli, Tiranti;
the church it seems and the pawnshop are not to be restored.

And so? A way a lone a last the
long loved street to watch the windless fall
of plane leaves clutch the pavements like severed swans feet
is this to be for a sign? this all

back, here, now, in the street; the houses like minipalazzi
a canal has dried up on; no footstep on a stair,
those stony stairs; no light in a third floor window
on this street where everything happened: a marriage a birth a war.

. . ./

For here of a Sunday morning two peaceful sleepers
who had overslept their peace were wakened by a bell
tinkling rather than tolling but tolling and telling
the shifty thirties were ending to the sound of a muffin bell

rung by a rubber booted masked a snouted
helmeted brave, an Oilskin, goggling in the sun
dredged from the private depths of a fetishist's dream book
to publicise a war the surrealists won.

When the house fell flat but the pan in the third floor bathroom
refused to be budged and stuck there back to the wall
in a bland and brave suspension of its natural function
for the long duration; an example to us all.

On that eve of ice and fire: year's end a world's end
when over a rubble of images gutterings sheds
a lustre of leaden tears and out of the steeples
the rafters flew like rooks and fell down dead.

But in the Bloomsbury basements the birds and the wind and the
    weather
planted arbours of rosebay where of an all clear night
the moon surprised the dried out souls of housemaids
criticizing Mr Eliot's poems by its dim Laforgueian light.

'Histories, histories. Everyone has them.
One is there one will listen. Reminiscence fades
like smoke through rain in lamplight. See.' I see my shadow
under the lamp acceptable to the shades

haunt here this street, these streets, these

'Streets. Where else? Who but his shadow with him?
Streets courts entries passages; a shady district known
all the hours on a clock; in darkness in flames in moonlight
and now, as it is now, at the dead time

the hermaphrodite hour. The season too and the weather
good hunting weather this, familiar ground;
the lamps in a looming mist, neon guttering rainbows
over flat stretches of asphalt and

. . ./

these same their empty pavements where without fear of trespass
their manor their village their parish, through which we moved
    widdershins:
out of a clockwise world where the spirits moved us
among them the named the known the loved

the dead. Haunt here this street. O tu che vai
under this lamp the shadow; who will come?
Summon them stranger now, the once that came unbidden,
one, is there one, one. Yes there was one.

Who was Sylvia, what was she, where drifted?
Decades and circles adrift from the high Edwardian rooms
scented with tuberose where Sargent painted
the spoiled child's face, the bronze chrysanthemums.

Washed up on the rocky shore of a different island
from the island she harped on she ruled with her wicked spells
the brawls the beauty the scandals the column of co-respondents
the names she nibbled and dropped like peanut shells

on Kleinfeldt's floor. An aging a mortal Circe
clutching her gin like a jewel, another name
in a footnote (in brackets) mis-spelt by some hack resurrectionist
digging between the wars: the one who came

back: the one bonafide familiar
in the sudden cold, the deadlock; lit and framed
by two iron lamp post limits, spindled between them
as though she were somehow tethered, was chained

in a run: the space allowed here elsewhere;
hatless coatless blurred by perpetual rain
refused in the Wheatsheaf, thrown out of the fucking Marquis
a continuous silent sequence: insult, rejection, blame.

Flickering out in the darkness flowed between them
a glimmer, a premonition; where he was placed and why
he was brought to this pass: omissions, denials, refusals;
five minutes he might have listened. A drink he did not buy.'

VII

Sister Anne,
Sister Anne?

Only the empty street
and the roofs in the rain.

Sister Anne?

Only the trees in the wind
the empty street
and the roofs in the rain.

Sister Anne,
Sister Anne?

Only a falling leaf,
the trees in the wind
and the roofs in the rain.

Sister Anne?
Only a crying child
and a falling leaf
and the roofs in the rain.

Sister Anne,
Sister Anne?

Only a crying child
and a mongrel dog
and the roofs in the rain.

Sister Anne?

Only a mongrel dog
and the falling leaves
and the roofs in the rain.

Sister Anne,
Sister Anne?

                                    . . ./

Only an empty street
and the trees in the wind
and the roofs in the rain.

Sister Anne?

Only an empty street
and –

*(Fatima opens the door. Bluebeard with sword and skull. Fatima
sinks down on her knees. Sister Anne cackles with laughter.)*

Eyes Wide Open

I used to dream for fun
how Love would come to one:
tall, rather shy and slim,
that's how I pictured him –
Oh how unwise:
Gosh, Mr Theodopopoulos
you opened my eyes.

I thought, I must confess,
Love would wear evening dress;
ever so debonair –
now I know love can wear
another guise:
Gosh, Mr Theodopopoulos
you opened my eyes.

The way I had it planned
he'd bend and kiss my hand;
speak softly in my ear
but not, oh dear, oh dear,
those hideous cries:
Gosh, Mr Theodopopoulos
you opened my eyes.

Love was to come my way
to end a perfect day:
I never had a hunch
it would be after lunch:
what a surprise:
Gosh, Mr Theodopopoulos
you opened my eyes.

A Near Thing

Fetch me the pistols, Alfred;
no; I don't know where they are:
look in the Louis Quinze commode
or the Fabergé samovar:
and put in a selection of bullets,
I'm afraid I don't know the way,
but Rose refused me twice last night
I must shoot myself once today.

You're in rather a hurry, Alfred:
the glasses are there, for two:
oh, anything pre-phylloxera,
the chateau d'Yquem will do;
and now: when you hear the pistol crack
and the thud on the bathroom door,
ring Rose and the *Times*; her number
is Wapping double four.

Those crocodile tears can dry now:
for God's sake here, take mine;
you won't improve your make up
and you'll certainly ruin the wine:
I sympathize with your feelings
and if it will help just a bit,
you can have what you've left of my wardrobe,
I know you know it will fit.

I insist that Sir Alfred Munnings
has my horse by Henry Moore:
if you could redeem my cuff links
distribute them to the poor:
just one more glass; and Alfred,
if you promise to look less glum
you can give my Francis Bacon
to that woman you say is your Mum.

.../

A vulgarian at heart.

Go get the pistols, Alfred;
(Alfred goes.)   ask cook for a carving knife;
the nineteenth baronet ends it all:
Rose: you rumpled a life
was smooth as a Betjeman poem
girl graduates murmur aloud;
now I sit like a chapel ruin
under a Piper cloud.

(con amore)   Dear Rose: that impossible party
with the kindergarten crew;
they were prospecting the Prospect
but there beyond Prospect, you;
wedged by an amateur matelot
and an unremarkable tart
you sat drinking port and guinness
and I sat eating my heart.

Her bed, the East India, there she lies a pearl.

Dear Rose, la belle tenebreuse,
you sound even better in French;
at last I said I adore you
and, darling, you said, 'Don't mench';
and I said to you: 'May I find you a drink';
and you said, 'Another of those';
and then you duskily murmured,
'They call me English Rose.'

(Telephone)   Ah, Alfred; clever to find them:
I'll take it myself; the last.
Yes, YES. YES, YES. YES get a taxi,
a taxi and get it fast:
oh, lend me some cash and drop them
and get in two dozen of stout:
Rose has been pinched robbing Woolworth's
and she wants me to bail her out.

Case History

She enters in a tutu, dancing dispiritedly and carrying
a mirror. 'I say, chaps, d'you mind if I sit down. Thank you
so much. It's my feet. Tagliovska's the name, née Putt. And
sometimes I wish I'd stayed Putt.'

My history as all histories are
is all the fault of my Mama
who, this is before I was born
was once a huntress with the Quorn;
till suddenly the silly goose
went mad about the Ballet Russe
and sometime before I was due
she settled in S.W.
It's my belief she must have gone
to l'après midi with a faun
for by the time she'd seen Petrouchka
she was already my mamouska.

She sings: examining herself in the mirror:

I like my hair,
my skin's quite good;
my teeth my own,
my health is rude;
I don't dislike my nose: it's rather sweet:
I hate my feet.

D'you mind if I remain seated: thank you so much.

According to my maiden aunt
I wore a tutu at the font
where, seeing how I was attired
my Daddie, Major Putt expired:
and long before the age of twelve
I'd been a bunny and an elve
a butterfly, a bouncing ball
and things too ghastly to recall.
Not to prolong this rigmarole
I then was sent to Wookey Hole;
Madame Kochantzchina you know
had there her famous studio,

...*/*

to learn with other lumping girls
that life is not a string of pearls.
Madame when we got on her wick
would beat us with a hockey stick
and swear at us in Portuguese:
besides the studio had fleas.
She sings:
I like my eyes
they're big and blue;
my nails are clean
my habits too;
I like my ears; I think they're rather sweet;
I hate my feet.
D'you mind if I take them off: my shoes I mean. Thanks awfully.
Is there a chiropodist in the house?
One day when I was at the barre
she threw at me the samovar,
a rather bitchy thing to do
or so at least I thought, don't you?
I threw it back; then joined a troupe
which brought the dance to Guadeloupe,
and me a fate far worse than death;
but rather fun; quite out of breath
I hurried back to Sadler's Well
where I created Merry Hell:
a major work by Oge Hist
the Swedish psychoanalyst
music by Beethoven and Balfe,
and costumes by a girl called Alf:
the whole thing was a ghastly mess
and a spectacular success.

She sings:
I love to sew
quite like to knit;
don't mind so long
as I can sit:
I've loved this little chat; it's been a treat
I hate my feet.

She gives a taxi whistle. 'Albrecht.' And is borne off by
a dreary boy in tights and jerkin; piggy back.

Ballad for the Dead Dancers

Now when the dawn is breaking,
round me a world is waking;
still the delight and music of night
invite to the dance.
Far from my dreams I wander,
hand in the hand of wonder,
nothing will fade, the words that she said,
the smile and the glance.
Dreaming I stand, a child between night and morning,
music that made my heart unafraid now whispers a warning:
faltering, changing, crying,
closer to silence sighing,
others there were, as young and more fair
whose life was the dance.

Where do they now lie sleeping?
deep in a spell whose keeping
no Prince can break to kiss them awake;
oh, where are they gone?
in the enchanted forest
she who was first and fairest,
Anna whose name was music and flame
who died like the swan.
Where are they now? oh soft as a sigh the answer,
swift though they were and light as the air, Death too is a dancer;
even though music beckon, only a ghost will waken
sadly and slow, as frail as the snow
as cold as the dawn
                    The Dance.
Where are they now? oh soft as a sigh the answer,
swift though they were and light as the air, Death too is a dancer,
Child by a ghost befriended, sister whose dance is ended,
warm from my breast I lay on your rest, the shade of a rose.

High in the pines the winds are sighing,
the winds of autumn stir the grass;
beyond the pines the waves replying
that seasons end and summers pass;
where lovers walked the walks are silent,
no voice but mine could break the spell:
the sea, the wind, the walks, the pinewoods;
you knew them all; you knew me well.

I was the voice
of every summer;
I sang you songs
of holidays;
I left with you
when they were over
some easy tune,
a simple phrase:
it was my songs your hearts were singing
when you were silent, holding hands;
filled with that old, that utter magic,
the songs I sang you on the sands.

Here were the chairs and there the footlights,
the old piano tinkling shrill;
and here I stood to sing my chorus
and there you sat around the hill:
I told you jokes as old as laughter,
your happy voices sang their part,
I knew you all when you were children,
I come again to touch your heart.

I was the voice
of all your summers,
I set the sun
and waves to rhyme;
I was the voice
of dusk and starlight,
the summer grass,
the scent of thyme;
I knew the words to fit the music

                                        .../

that every young heart understands;
filled with that old, that utter magic,
the songs I sang you on the sands.

I was the voice
of all your summers;
I sang you songs
of holidays;
I leave you still
now summer's over,
that easy tune,
that simple phrase:
I am the voice your heart remembers
in sadder times, in other lands;
and still at night you sing your children
the songs I sang you on the sands.

VIII

The First Fabliau
Else a great prince in prison lies.

The minor prince his stupid counsellors gone
(but wise enough to know which way a gun
is pointing) over to the generals
runs wild and free; a day of opened doors
and flights and landings along corridors
up stony stairs where from their burial
at birth in carpets his feet rise and fall
in love with footsteps, until tired he tries
ungilded chairs beds without canopies
stiff straw for heroes. Here our hero lies.
Erect and sword in hand while church bells ring
over the gallows where the generals swing –

he tiptoes up, behind a dirty pane
puts out his tongue at sentries in the rain.

Then sleeps. Another day. And now he must
come down to carpets and to carpet's dust,
through shuttered sheeted drawingrooms he must run
and run he does the gauntlet of his glum
resplendent and redundant ancestors
into the throne room. The great double doors
sigh shut. A cat is sitting on the throne
and does not look at him, he feels alone
divested, mean, and to uncrown it all
which way he looks a mirror on a wall
presents a common and divested thing
that pulls the very face he pulled, at him.

Down to the depths. But for a fallen king
how far is fallen. Bedrock is the thing:
on the stair's last step he'll abdicate
find him a cell and so he does; too late.
Too late. A eunuch dwarf by that same door
down the same stairs, but faster, years before
and none too soon for guns were pointing fled
from the bedchamber and the bed. The Bed.

. . ./

To live; by holding his angelic tongue
unfed unhappy but, take heart, not hung
who now at least the cooks and scullions gone
can sample swill and pick himself a bone
and find a cell to rest and entertain
a Visitor and offer him; champagne.

The dungeons sunk to cellars long ago
rack Rehoboams row on row on row.

He sips in silence but such grace; such grace;
makes speech a cruel distortion of the face.
He is himself his message. More champagne
for this fair guest the fairest guest since when
since angels elsewhere once and they were dim,
as Lot was barbarous, compared to him.

Compared to him compared; compared to whom
this sudden Someone, that's for certain, come
from Somewhere. Why? The eunuch has to know
the dwarf is undecided so they go
down on one knee, it hurts, and fails to please
their cagey guest. Nothing as bent as knees.
Chastened by hiccups he extends his hand,
fervently kissed, then feeling odd but grand
and ravenous, He exerts the royal will
stamps on a flag stone begs it to lie still
takes three steps back to show He can then goes
this way and that following his nose.
Breakfast is cooking and a table laid
but will he reach it before grace is said
will there be time to grope and skid and guess
through halflit stillrooms pantries kitchens. Yes.

A naked bulb hangs down. No single light
has ever shown so much not meant for sight,
dumped down piled up swept over kicked about
cracked broken parted holed stove in burned out
pots crocks tubs barrels bags the makeshift bins
for crusts bones feathers innards peelings skins;
but one clear space there is, one half veiled shrine

.../

by smalls and dishcloths sagging on a line
where Venus stands, flushed from the reeking stove
and bobs a welcome to her dim alcove.

This curtsey is no garden party trick
cooks if not curtsied are apt to kick.

He bows. She giggles. He is not surprised. Surprise
is never shown a goddess in disguise
besides he's not a bit surprised he knows
that when a Goddess goes to earth. She goes.
Much like a prince would in masquerade
he'd be a groom she'll be a serving maid
no prince or goddess would descend to pass
Himself or Herself off as middle class.
Nor does she does she but before it burns
she ups the smoking frying pan and turns
its offering on a plate, one cracked, cold, plate.
Do as the Gods do. Use your fingers mate.
Two hot dropped mouthfuls and their hands resign
from work so coarse, their fingers are too fine,
let stomachs starve, and fly for comfort where
they touch and taper to a point of prayer
that bows their head and catches their sweet breath
and closes up his eyes, can this be death
the eunuchs wine and kiss: he cannot bear
his shirt and tunic, armour stuffed with hair,
he must go naked or he will be dead.

                                    She lifts her head.

Unclasps his collar. Ah. As though she knew
the mischief undone buttons can undo
and studs and buckles stud and buckle give
the swaddling bands are loosening. Will he live?
Whose life may hang on one last stubborn fly?
She'll to the root and cure. He will not die.
He will not die far past a death it is
more than a cure a metamorphosis
the earth bound grub mounts on the wings of change
to service flowers and finds it no more strange
than he to bend and with bare hands undo

                                            . . ./

73

for the first time the lacing of a shoe
which time enough for her to shrug away
those rags this apron served her yesterday
discarded shadows out of which she steps
two paces to the right: and pirouettes.

So one mad midnight the astronomer
saw through his glass a somersaulting star.

Now are they naked both as God them meant
who made them fair and made them different
and where they differ most they most agree
leave the dull mind to ask them, after, why.
Not why they meet but why they met so late
and how they did when they were separate
must soon be joined together; he and she,
a law unto themselves: ourselves to be
together and alone. First mice obey
and creep into their holes and there they stay
quiet as mice. Firebrat and silver fish
crowd with the cockroach underneath one dish,
maggots whose food is motion do not move
content to hunger if not die for love.
No spider spins and small lascivious flies
close in despair a multitude of eyes
to douse the light as though two children slept
dreaming an unrecorded dream. Except.

Except a caged bird she had meant to free
but kept because it kept her company,
she sang to it because it would not sing,
hops on its idle perch the cockbird king
set young buds dancing to a song he made
on the green twig before the lime was laid;
to sing for her her silence clear and far
like the late thrush that hails the first lit star
Vesper adest; and who but he to hail
the right true end of love and end this tale
for us but not for him and not for long.

How many variations has a song?

IX

Salathiel's Song

I was born between night and morning
on a crooked road from there to the next place:
the portents were usual
a commotion of cockerels and comets
a parish of barking dogs.

My name is Salathiel.
I named myself.
Naked I knelt by the christening stream
I called my name   an echo answered
echoes and apparitions have always been kind.

My father was a Magician
in a small way.
He left me,
the doves alas were dead,
in a battered tea chest:
two decks of cards
with three jacks missing
four foreign coins
seven dog eared almanacs
in a battered tea chest
his crumpled nibbled
charts of the sky and the skull,
unlucky joker,
of the left hand palm.
In a battered tea chest
smelling of mice and time
his riddled spells
unstoppered phials
Elixir's dust.

His last words were:
                    'Get out of magic.'
Where to?
                    What else?
A lumbering wagon
on country roads rocking the linnets' cages
                                        . . ./

cradled my cradle.
I was suckled on milk and clouds
I was weaned on wormwood.
The colours of smoke
the sounds of water
the smell of tarpaulin
the taste of sorrel:
four simple lessons still unlearned.

That ribbon of smoke
across the valley
is a road we climb.

That plod of hooves
when loads are heavy
is water clopping into a pail.

The whisper of water
this side of silence
is green fire lighted
under a pot.

In a field by a stream.
When the mares were watered
the shadows of elms
came down to drink.

An hour before sunset
the fire was lighted
is embers now.
The cauldron scoured.

A day has closed
like a shut accordion.
The lanterns doused.

A watchdog howls
across the valley.
An owl asks why.

. . ./

On a crooked road
from there to the next place
the travellers sleeping
their lurchers sleep.

Children asleep.
But one child watches
the embers die.

Dark elm
far owl
faint star
my mother
my mother dark as the night.

Your candles burn. A man walking the roads.

What man this late?

You know the man I mean.
He walked the roads at fair and harvest time
slept in the barns, worked sometimes, or he begged.

Many such men.

You know the man I mean. Because he knew
two tags of Latin and a ballad tune
he must be Merlin, Merlin the Wild, or else
Thomas the Rhymer, Thomas of Erceldoune,
True Thomas.

Let him sleep: sleep under Eildon.
Why waken him?

You waken him. Night after night
your candles burn on starheight on the hill.
You summon him, not I.
Out of the moonless mediaeval dark
to the bare chamber and the tressel board
where the novitiate in the school of night
studies his book.

What book?

The bare unwritten page.

Eliots Armstrangs and Johnsons ride
thieves a'

The great gates fallen.

Not a stone or post
stands up to mark where once
the wall's circumference ran.
Avenue and path are lost
where the horsemen rode abreast
now a hound must fight its way
to that hospitable hearth
where till dawn the leveret lay.

Form where a hare has lain
at dawn above the stream
a heron haunts at dusk.
A dream drives out a dream.
The heron and the hare
are these his revenants?
The eagle and the fox.
Eagle and fox might share
between them his terrain;
bog crag scrub moorland moss
his cunning and his pride
who built a peelhouse here
over the border side.

Half cowshed half a throne.
Twice razed, the fox rebuilt
above the brawling linn
his eyrie and grew old
brooding: a spear at rest:
old scores ill faith bad blood
blood where the wine was spilt
blood where the ford runs cold.
Bed ridden at the last
did some cramped ague night
long mounting fever fledge
out from that rough nest

. . ./

in broadest daylight air
a territorial claim
so long as woods shall grow
or waters run: a dream.
The windows to the west
outgazing on a long
prospect of peace a dream
the shadows on the lake
lit by a summer dawn
embrasures battlements;
gifts to delight the swan.

He would have dreamed a dream.

He who had dreamed his dream
out of a leveret's bed
and lucky to lie there
lucky to leave; a man
half risen from the dead
a hunted broken man
could still find breath to swear:
by the five fords I crossed
the hairbreadth track I fled
and by the man I killed
here and no other place:
here and no other place
to build both hearth and stall
shelter for man and beast
a peelhouse and a wall.

The creaking hinge the falling glass
what's ever prone to ache or ail
under the weather, spoke of this
it is a time for gales, this gale
out of the west, as darkness fell
found its own voice and spoke to me
inland on this autumnal hill
of winter, anger and the sea.

That now through midnight seems to vent
the fury of an entire force
against this known impediment
of cob and thatch till all the doors
complain how latch and catch come loose
and grudge and give as though they must
desert their posts; let the old house
stable that stallion strength at last.

But the great beam from wall to wall
weathers another storm that broke
at summer's end before the fall
there in the raftered dark the oak
answers: erect among its peers
branching the long felled woodland mocks
with all its green affirmative years
the fury of the equinox.

Storm before storm; what storm gives tongue
in this delirium howls and raves
down through the night as night wears on
howled at the opened mouths of caves
issue of blood, the scent of birth
dogs him to death and man is back
a beast pursued and round its earth
old hounds are hunting with the pack.

.../

A morning loath to come to light
more muted than the dark was wild
muffled in cloud; inside and out
no barking dog no restive child
no footstep on the road, no sound
no earthly sound but from the sky
a seabird seaward homeward bound;
one harsh consolatory cry.

The long day's dusk revealed
low in the west and bright
a crescent moon and star
deepens till field and wood
Redlands and Eastern hill
darken into night.

Herdsmen what night is this?
This night on those dark hills
your first forefathers lit
on brae and tor and fell
north southward eastward west
nightlong midsummer fires
blazed as though earth beneath
mirrored the firmament
under the summer stars.

Harvesters herdsmen mourn
the unengendered spark
mourn the unkindled fire.
The flame the smoke the fire
the ash and ember, mourn;
how else shall flocks be healed
fields flourish and be fed
the orchards fructified?

Girls who danced garlanded, mourn;
striplings outleapt the flames
cold on the darkened hills
sad ghosts of summers past
mourn the midsummer fires.

But in a darkening room
barefooted, hushed, a boy
kneels to his task, to light,
cupping his slender hands,
tall candles stand erect
two tall white candles make
an altar of the hearth
and consecrate the fire.

.../

What fire is this?

                               The fire I lit
was that midsummer fire dark years ago
the infidel put out: but he and I
last of our order, true believers both
rekindle under vows and when it dies
we come like pilgrims to the orchard here
and where we knelt must kneel
to rise twin keepers of the Sacred Grove
welcomes tonight, this night, the dispossessed
spirits of trees and streams who walk invisible
whom we alone can hear: like foxgloves fingered
silk caressing silk seducing silence
till the breathless dark rustles and whispers
Night. Midsummer night. Tonight the fern
will seed itself at midnight. Midnight comes
see how the fronds are changing: amber into gold
and gold to flame fathering a thousand sparks
scatter and fall like stars and where they fall
lost treasure shines and the sad shadows dance.

Leda Poem

To borrow a torch
for a dark lane:
this is reasonable.

To hoist to the kitchen lamp
(cupped in careful hands)
an outsize EGG:
this could be explained.

Under that swaddle of feathers
those delusions of gander
the flesh was goose
all goose.

A satisfactory outcome
I hear you say.
Do say.
By all means say.

But remember; remember:

That 'look what I've got'
in the kitchen doorway.

Those upheld hands
that precocious fondling.

The muddy jeans
the keepsake feather.

And consider, consider:

The celestial sightings
by mundane observers.

That clamour of wings
you could set your watch by.

. . ./

Those majestical threshings
of small domestic ponds.

O lady, lady
there are only two ways about it:
either you cook a fabulous omelet
or you've laid yourself in for
an epic load of trouble.

Peacocks

I would be Adam
leafless in the garden
with all my ribs about me
one day more.
For one more day
the Voice be off the air:
a Heavenly silence
in which I find my feet
and flex my fingers
to grasp the Situation.

I doan like it.

To be creation's clown
a six day wonder
a ten toed bi-ped
with this bag of pebbles
that wobble when I walk.

He should have held his breath.
Five days was plenty.
Earth, sea, beasts, fowl; then feet up.

Make feathers fly and finish.

Peacocks.
Full stop.

Peacocks was really great.

In Memoriam

He was born
Moammed Sceab.

A scion of emirs
of nomads.
He died,
he killed himself
in Paris,
because he belonged
nowhere.

He loved France
and so he changed his name.

He became Marcel
but he was no Frenchman

and no place for him now
in the tents of his tribe
listening
among his kinsmen
to the song of the Prophet,
sipping his coffee.

And his own song
the song of a man
alone, elsewhere,
never to be sung.

He is buried in Ivry.
Ivry
that ramshackle suburb
like a fairground
falling to bits.

...../

I was a mourner.
Myself and the landlady
of the house where we lodged.
5 rue des Carmes
run down downhill alley.

And I, now maybe I
alone among the living
to tell you
he lived.

after Giuseppe Ungaretti

Exegi.
I have brought to perfection.
Monumentum.
A monument
outbrazening bronze
upstaging the pyramids
windproof weatherproof
spondees and dactyls
which not the no, nor the next
nor the subsequent centuries
centuries
centuries
shall.

   PFUI

Preserve what was frigid from birth
in a deep happy frozen hereafter.
Which leaves me perishing cold,

But warm
but warm for the transient
the here and the gone;
things going my way
all in one boat, one boatman.
Easy, you say, to come by?
But come by not to keep.

Take a song.
Take a song for example a song
sung in the summer shows
was pounded
by four bit bands
to dust in provincial palais
and was introduced to the West
by a busker
working the theatre queues.

                        .../

Until one morning
one autumn morning the milkman
whistling its opening bars
in his doorstep to doorstep medley
signalled a final rendition
by a glacial crescendo of empties.

But a plane tree in the square
secure between its summers
scattered a handful of leaves
over urban flagstones
far from the padlocked pavilions
the shuttered resorts of summer
and the rough unsurfable sea.

'But an old man can summon
shadows to his side
or they may come unbidden.'
How well I guessed what I lived long to learn
and now at last I know.
These shadows come
they come to us unbidden and they stay
through the long twilight with us till the dark;
remembered faces hide forgotten names
women and girls: that girl, one girl, the girl

the girl who went mad.
In autumn it was
that autumn the sirens
wailed over rooftops their warning
to a city of silenced bells.

She walked the familiar street
scanning each square of pavement
engrossed in a childish game
a game she played with death.

She walked the sunlit street
always this far no farther
and always behind her
walked the twin shadows her warders
the length of a prison yard.
She walked the long straight street
her lips continually moving
to voices not her own.

Day after day
she walked the street.
When I saw her
I crossed to the other side
and was ashamed.

. . ./

And now.
And now the remembered face; the light loose hair
darkened by autumn rain; the summer dress
torn at the hem and trailing. Herself as she was.

Herself as she was.

Herself as she was
the king's most beautiful daughter
the girl who went mad, possessed
by the gift of a God who had loved her;
the knowledge she has to foretell
to those who will not believe her;
the message as welcome as death
that fire is the fate of cities.

Remembering childhood now
when I am old
is to recall old men
my childhood knew.

Old country men who taught a country boy
to listen and to look: the moorland calls
of quail and curlew; on the stony field
the peewit's nest; the fox pad in the snow.
Lessons learned, his eyes and ears turn elsewhere.
He has seen Orion and the Bear, has heard
the voice of minstrels: men who tramp the roads
and sleep in barns. Hirds who walk their flocks
over the border from the English side
and talk in thees and thous. The solitary man
dwarfed by his stallion, a four footed God
tremendous in the dusk.
Travellers all and all with tales to tell.

Silence for Mr Pape.

For Mr Pape we must a journey take
over the viaduct: stations on our way
are read in flowers and shells.
The terminus is summer and the sea.
The days are sand and plimsolls.
The nights are his. Together side by side
we sit on upturned boxes in the yard.
He speaks. I listen. In the fading light
roundabout music from the distant fair
provides accompaniment: to ragtime tunes
we march together through the Golden Gate
into the Golden West we pick our way
through orange groves so bright and tangible
that when the moon, a ripe full August moon
has cleared the rooftops
I reach up my hand.

So many come and gone.
How few are left: so few
that this may be the last.
This spring, this early spring, the last.
These roadside celandines
these daffodils
of all your springs
with all their flowers, the last.

And first; flower of all flowers
from childhood on, the gean.
Seeded in Eden
the celestial tree.

The hawthorn petals
falling on our path
along Leith Water
lying where they fell.
The chimes at midnight
and the talk, of love.

The first mimosa on the market stalls.
Magnolias
camelias at Kew.
Flower on the black bough
flower on the green leaf.
The lilac branches
weighed down in the rain
over the garden railings in the square.

Helen in Kleinfeldts.
That year she wore
her Manet barmaid's hairdo.
Here began
her millinery phase.
A boy's straw boater lay, bedeckt,
bedaisied, periwinkled, white and blue
between us on the table.

.../

I laid my hand
over her outspread hand.
(She wore no rings.)
If they, she said, if they
pushed a piano
pushed a concert grand
an Erard pushed before me
I could play.

Late twenties? Early Thirties?
Take your pick.
And she; the girl you spoke of?
She died young. Now I forget
what year it was; but sometime in the spring.
She died in spring.
And music too.
preludes, mazurkas, nocturnes, barcarolles?
Some song, that summer, whistled in the street
played by one wayward finger.
What song, which summer, both of us forget.
The rest
is silence.

'The moon has set.'
Listen a woman is speaking

'The moon has gone down
And the Pleiades'

In an early dialect
of a dead language
a woman is speaking

The muse herself is speaking

The moon has set
and the Pleiades.
Midnight.
The watchman has passed.

And I sleep alone.

Darkness. The wind nightlong
the sea till daybreak
loud on the headland.
The island voices
sea and wind together.
No other,

No other?

This was the dream
long years of dreams ago.
Tonight I hear it still.

This is the dream.
A summer morning early
after long absence walking as I would
this road of all roads first; past the lodge gates
and following the wall was overhung with laurels;
laurels overhang: nothing has changed.
Beechwood and birdsong everything remembered
until the bridge in sight, between its stones
out of forgottenness the yarrow flowers
my childhood flowers and like a child I run
to lean and look and listen.
Leaned and looked
at silence: looked at stones
between green banks had been the river bed
and made a river's music. Night and day.
Ground bass at morning to the songs of birds
since birds perfected song. The last hoarse voice
of summer evenings across silent fields
to hush a child asleep.

How long, dream time how long, before the change?
The river stones have darkened. From the bank
clutching a hazel branch I lean
out over water rising to a flood
sunlit and crystal clear, transparent as the wind
loud as the wind and in its lucid depth
like a green branch belaboured by a storm
a clump of grass makes visible the force
sweeps us away.

                    I wakened in the dark
to lie in darkness listening to the dream
that would not let me sleep. A captive child
has heard secreted in the whorled shell
an unbeknown unsilenceable sea.

Thrush
for Louis Johnson

An odd couple
man and boy
alone in the house together.

The child in his cot.
The man in a chair close by.
Eighty years between them.

The boy asleep.
The man afeard,

that the dogs will bark in the yard.
The rooks erupt in the spinney
and the child will waken and cry.

(A fear nigh fifty years old
from a winter after a war,
a bitter winter it was,
and a child who would not be comforted.)

A jet flies low overhead.
The child does not waken;
slowly, serenely
he turns his head to his minder
not to be reassured
but rather to reassure him.

Now they meet face to face.

Two they are of a kind
transmigrant
each with a journey before him
whereto neither can know.

...\

I on the sparrow's path
down, under the shadow of Orcus
from which no swallow returns
not the quail nor the corncrake.

And you.
But you, the bambino
once must have lain on the lap
of a quattrocento Madonna
now down to earth again
a barefoot beginner.

A blond and barefooted beginner.

How shall I? Help me here. Whisper it. What can I
what can I give to a child
in farewell? Softly, speak softly.
In farewell to a child who is sleeping
give?

What can I give but a dream?

But a dream is no dream when you waken
into the morning you dreamed of;
its sunlight its blossom its birdsong.

Listen, Louis, the thrush
your thrush
but nearer now clearer now
high on a chosen tree top
to sing you his twice over song.

Sing oak sing ash sing elder and apple and alder
woodland and ploughland and redland; he sings what he sees:
a landscape, a lane through a landscape
will father your footsteps your first steps
and lead you:

. . ./

will lead you
from garden to spinney from spinney to orchard
from primrose to dog rose from orchard to meadow
from foxglove to foxglove from meadow to river
and there:
there in the summer rain a heron will rise from the shallows
spreading great wings heavy with acclamation
and the thrush will end his song.

X

Give the tree a shake
who tumbles down?
Old song for his supper's sake
an Adam an angry man;
bow in bony hand
his fiddle under his chin
ready to take his stand
at a kirn or hiring fair
at a penny wedding or wake
or kerbed on the market square.
All for his supper's sake.
Twopenny worth of gin
clean straw thrown in for a bed
his fiddle under his chin
his tunes tucked up in his head
reel and schottische and strathspey
if the dancers dropped down dead
on the floors of the barn he could play
airs without end Amen
jigs for judgement day:
bow in bony hand
that stuttering limp of a squint
could wheedle drink from a stone
with a tongue would blacken a saint
that old light fingered clown
who,
if you,
tumbles down.

Show me a man and I'll raise you a devil
in a preacher's frock or a soldier's coat:
there's no religion under the navel
said the old woman
the wise old woman
the old wise woman at Folly Gate.

When I was young the lounging sun
was my companion time to spend;
but all the times we tossed he won
my false inseparable friend.

I have been happy in a dive
between the radio and the rain
O frequent lives that I shall never live
and castles further off than Spain.

A tabby fiddle and a tom guitar
'There came a man a man from out the south'
have made such music in my drunken ear
I have been happy in a bankrupt bar
as I discovered and forgot the truth.

I have been happy watching happiness
visit a room as simply as the sun
turning a gesture into a caress
and turning every sentence to a song.

Honour the forebears of your starry trade
unbriefed computerless alas who now
but Liam's shadow or else Nina's shade
count down at Kleinfeldts steer towards the Plough.

Whaur's Isadora Duncan dancin noo?
Whaur's Mary Garden aince was Mélisande?
Damned if I know but is the old man fou
and has he still the thistle in his hand?

Where was that face foreseen?
The golden age gone by:
Goddess, Protectress, Queen
what smith in Syracuse
dreaming antiquity;
carved on the obverse die
his last prophetic trace,
Goddess, Protectress, Muse
with backward looking eye;
and so foresaw her face.

Who would read me 'au soir à la chandelle',
when they are old, grown old, careless of cheek and hair?
Would Helen read me or would Isabel,
who once were fair and dark; my dark, my fair.

To read my hand and find I have no heart
is doubtful palmistry but honest thieving
and true. I have no heart if finding's keeping
I know I had one. Losing is believing.

And now will you believe me when I tell you
it is a heart so you will not confuse it
with idle severed things; cut curls, loose jewels.
It is my heart and yours. For God's sake use it.

Hide it a place with oil and food and lotion.
Who knows; the table with a saint's bone under
rises an altar; so this sulking kernel
may run sweet oil for you and work its wonder.

Pray on it then alone before your mirror
where women pray, to end a separation
which makes a relic of my heart and elsewheres
and martyrs me. It is a false vocation.

Reviens, reviens, cher ami,
seul ami, reviens. Je te jure
que je serai bon.

Who has not heard that cry?
Come back I will be kind.
How could you dream that I
what comfort will you find
alone adrift apart
come back my love, my dear
how could you leave me here
broke with a broken heart.

Is it days, hours, is it years?
I cannot sleep or think
or eat or count or drink
everything tastes of tears.
No news from you? What news?
I've pawned your last two shirts
I've got to wear your shoes
and now my left foot hurts.

Reply reply reply.
My love what will you do?
I think only of you.
Who has not cried that cry?
We are unique, a pair
measured matched aligned:
come back my love I swear
I swear I will be kind.

War and winter wait for us
strangers in a shabby room
hushed like thieves have stumbled on
Time's unguarded treasure house.
All the pasts we did not share
what the future meant to keep
heaped around us till we kneel
half from love but half in prayer.

That the night which brought us here
time and continents apart
side by side the narrow stair
to this summit: where the heart
clear in all its regions lay
landscaped by our happiness:
that this night may others bless.

And be the night the miser find
long where lost his jewel lies.
Folly wear her best disguise.
And to listening ears the dumb
speak the visions of the blind.
Night when no child grieves, a night
lucky for thieves
for homeless lovers, home.

'When was it first,' she said.
'The day we walked together
pilgrims to the Spring
in the April Easter weather
when the lily and the gean
were carpet and canopy
the flower before the leaf
the leaf a mist of green
that hung about the thorn:
but every bush and tree
a seignory of song
song soaring over song
promise on prophecy.
The prophecy our wine
the promise was our bread.'
'Was it then, was it then,' she said.

'Not then, not then,' he said.
'There was a night together
in the fall of rain and leaf
late through the wind and weather
when on the broken walls
of the empty terraces
the shadows implored like ghosts
of the wind tormented trees
like ghosts denied their rest.
But on the crest of the wind
rose the incoming year
to tide us beyond our grief
to shore us above our fear.
And out of the reach of the dead.'
'It was then, it was then,' he said.

To loathe and love. How comes it? Hear the heart
lost for an answer tear itself apart.

This is the story of a little pin
who wanted to be a kilderkin.

The candles yawning and the fire gone out.
Silence, your sin; let silence make amends.
You will not write a line and if you wrote
what could you write but epitaphs and ends?

Say your say to earn the silence
soon must pay a lodge and bed
words will never win you. Settle.
And the worm be satisfied.

Not to be, not to be born is best
so the chorus sing.

Room for a beggar man.

What but a crown of thorn
could cap the suffering
marks out that wounded brow?

This man was once a king.
He begs no kingdom now.

A dark low ceilinged room
a single bed and rest.
Let the chorus sing
not to be born is best.

An old man a poor man
a poor old man alone.
Who was Agamemnon
a splinter of his bone;
and crafty Odysseus
was a morsel in his mind.
An old man a poor man
the poor old man was blind.

A poor man a blind man
so the story runs.
Gods were his confederates
and Heroes were his sons.
And Helen was his daughter
when she walked on the wall.
An old man a blind man
the father of us all.

Poets you may read it in
William Yeats or Hölderlin:
care for language, learn your trade
nothing is that is not made
made to stand, transparent, fine,
like the glass that holds the wine.

Seán Rafferty and Nicholas Johnson in Conversation

My great-grandfather, Hugh, came over from Killarney in the early 1800s and settled in Dumfriesshire. He married a farmer's daughter. I came of farming stock, highland and lowland. My mother was a MacGregor. When that clan was proscribed, her forebears came south to Ettrick and changed their name to Grieve. Eventually, they went back north to Perthshire. Sometimes when I was young, my mother would remind me that I was descended from Rob Roy. What to do? Run out into a field and steal a cow. All connection with Ireland was lost. The only Irishmen I knew were tramps who came over at certain times to find casual farm-work. I sat with them in the back yard while they drank tea. Some were educated men: 'two tags of Latin and a ballad tune'. I was given children's versions of Irish legends to read, so that Cuchulain and Conchubar shared my heroic dreams with Hector and Agamemnon and Kinmont Willie and Clym o' the Cleugh. But Cuchulain won with Kinmont Willie a close second. My father in his old age became more talkative. One day he said casually that our name wasn't Rafferty but Monteith. It was too late. My name was Rafferty and I was insolubly Irish.

The two lines in 'William Woolsery is Dead' – 'hares grow merry and by night / leap the long furrows in delight' – you wrote when you were eight or nine.

From my window I saw a jack hare leaping over furrows in moon-light. It was winter, bitterly cold. That stuck in my mind – as an image. Ours was a spartan house, cold: we had stone hot-water bottles. I would get up at seven in the morning to write. My sister and parents looked at my poems. Nobody told me what to read and what not to read... Mine was a lonely childhood. Of course, I went to the great fairs at Dumfries. I knew a girl who had a club foot, she was very pretty. I only saw her three times. But it was almost a fetish, this attraction I had for this contraption on her leg. When I was eleven, my parents gave me a fishing-rod. So I used to go down to the river and fish.

What poetry and prose did your parents or your sister recite to you as a child?

I don't think my mother knew much Gaelic, but she sang me songs

127

and lullabies in Gaelic and she played me reels and schottiches and strathspeys and jigs and pibrochs. My father who couldn't sing taught me to sing: 'Quand trois poules vont au champ / La première va devant.' He, an abstemious man, also taught me: 'The rising moon began to glower / The distant Cumnock hills oot ower.' My sister who was five years older insisted on my learning chunks of *The Golden Treasury* which I can still recite if anyone would like to listen.

There were a lot of French books in the house, mostly novels. One such began with the line: 'Ah qu'ils sont triste ces soirs d'Octobre.' I was hooked. There was also a French translation of *War and Peace*. By the time I had finished that – well, nearly finished it – I had quite a good French vocabulary.

I'm surprised, reading my poems, how many biblical references there are. Sharon, Siloam, Cain and Eve, the angels camping around in Sodom. But of course we went to church every Sunday: at school we went twice. It was agonisingly boring.

What do you think of the Scottish language?

As a small boy in a country parish I spoke it, the lowland variant, with a vocabulary and construction of its own. I think it's a wonderful language: argumentative, funny, tender. I don't think I would ever have written in Lallans though those early short poems of MacDiarmid's are magical. I was born in a literary neck: Carlyle four miles down the road; Burns in Dumfries where I went to school. An old lady who was a direct descendant of Burns used to walk about trying to pat small boys on the head but I was too quick for her. And Gareth Langholm.

Describe Edinburgh.

The path along Leith water. The Water of Leith is, was, a small polluted stream that trickled between abandoned perambulators, bicycle frames, bedsteads, under the Dean bridge: Telford's miraculous bridge, a single shaft soaring out of the narrow gorge. We went there to talk under the trees on summer nights after the pubs had shut. We? Three or four medical students, American medical students, Polish German Jewish American students; a Russian, also a medical student, born in Petersburg which he left when he was ten: and because the Russian was there, by a stroke of luck, me. And so I am sitting on a low stone wall picking hawthorn petals off my trousers as they fall. I am nineteen. Round and above me on the summer night float the recurrent now-comprehensible names: Dostoevsky, Nietzsche, Schopenhauer, Ouspensky. I am slightly drunk. A blind American-Pole like an anorexic Jesus is teaching me, with special attention to vowels, 'Buffalo Bill's defunct'. I am happier than I have ever been.

Although the Russians had been in translation for years maybe it was in the twenties that Dostoevsky and Chekhov took off. I still read the last pages of *Karamazov*: Ilyusha's funeral. Later with the Russian I heard Pushkin, Mayakovski and Essenin. We drank Scotch from bits of china, presents from Troon, from the mantelpiece of his lodgings. And there was music too from our joint gramophone. *Petrouchka, Petrouchka, Petrouchka*.

The time I was there – there was a kind of aristocracy of lawyers, they were the reigning monarchs. In Edinburgh the professor of music was called Donald Tovey. Every Sunday night during the winter he gave public lectures with illustrations on the piano. I learned a lot from that.

Were you very poor when you were in Edinburgh?

Oh no. I wasn't poor. The family helped. And I got a scholarship.

Apart from music in poetry, is there music in song which has inspired you?

Well, it would have begun with Burns. In the ballads – Thomas the Rhymer – there were five or six of the great ballads, and the *Reliques*. One was 'Adam Bell, Clym o' the Clough, and William of Cloudesly' who slaughtered half the population of Carlisle by themselves.

In London and Devonshire, writing for musicals, do you think you learned from the ballads?

No. That came from working at 'The Players'; the Victorians, the nineteenth-century music hall. The thirties were full of Gershwin, Cole Porter, Django Reinhardt.

What was the literary scene in Edinburgh at the time?

I don't think it existed much when I began to write for *The Modern Scot*. I did get slightly mixed up with people who were vaguely mixed up with the Scots National Party. Well, I met MacDiarmid there.

Did you know 'The Drunk Man' and the early poems in 1930?

No. I'm not sure. I knew 'Penny Wheep' and the early poems then – but I can't remember – you see, for most of his life he was out of print.

Like you.

Yes. But it was my own fault really.

Do you consider yourself a Scottish poet?

No.

English?

No.

Irish?

Leave the Irish bit…it's ridiculous.

You used to hear Robert Garioch play piano in a cinema.

I went to this cinema to hear him play piano. This impressed me enormously. Only Garioch wasn't the name he used then. And he was a very nice guy.

And did you talk about poetry?

No. Because he didn't tell me he was writing.

What about Sir Herbert Grierson?

He was my professor. He did the great edition of Donne in 1910 – and I didn't go to the University until 27 or 28 and I think he'd rested on the great tradition of Donne. I was in his honours class and I was his best pupil and I never spoke to him. Quite extraordinary. He was a handsome man and he came from the Orkneys and had a

beautiful speaking voice and he recited us poetry sometimes.
Wyatt.

*Do you have strong recollections of writing poetry while you were in
Scotland?*

I enjoyed it more. Because it was all light verse really, and it came
quite easily.

You were passionate about cinema.

I go back to silent days. Ben Hur. Lillian Gish. Silent Garbo . . . I did
see some Russian films. The Communist Party showed them in an
infants' school. I don't know if I saw any Eisenstein then. Pabst
wouldn't have been shown. Not in Edinburgh. Pudovkin I saw.
That had an enormous effect on me. I only wish silent films had
gone on another ten years longer. Surely some of the silent films are
the nearest thing to poetry that there is.

What were your feelings about Eliot, Pound and Joyce?

Eliot means *The Waste Land*; Pound *Cathay, Hugh Selwyn
Mauberley* and *Homage to Sextus Propertius*. George Shiley who
was county librarian in Dumfries did as much for my education as
my teachers. One day he gave me a neatly wrapped book. When I
opened it there in its blue cover with the great black unstrung bow
was the Shakespeare *Ulysses*.

Why did you go to London?

Because it was a City. To get lost. I arrived there in 1932. I lived for
about a year in Hampstead. After then in Charlotte Street or
Fitzroy Street and the Square. I did live in Lambs Conduit Street.
The man in the flat above claimed to be the King of Poland so we
had the Polish flag floating above us and a Jewish deli in the ground
floor. Fitzroy Street was where I lived: nothing to do with Fitzrovia
or whatever that means.

Which poets influenced you during the 1930s?

The Metaphysicals: all of them, especially Donne and Herbert. It
was Herbert who stayed. They were in the air at the time and it was

131

from them as much as from the *Lyrical Ballads* that I learned plain speech. Dryden was in the air too: Homages to John Dryden. I read him too which was as well since I've written so much in couplets. I had been reading Yeats all through the Thirties so when I began writing poetry again his influence showed in poems like 'The Old Stag'. I wrote no poetry from around 1934 to 1940. I did write a novel, a novel and a half in fact. If I had stayed in Scotland would I have gone on writing poetry? I don't know. All my poetry seems to me to be about the common themes of poetry, death, childhood, places, story telling and a lot of it is in traditional forms and metres. When I began again I think the first poems were two for Christian [only child, b. 1940] and I am back with my old instructors, the metaphysicals. I did write poems some of which I have kept; it was all rather painful as though I were starting again from scratch.

Which French Symbolist poets had any influence?

Very little had any influence. But inspiration. They were great poets. On the night of the twenty-fourth of January I used to get down on my ancient knees and pray for de Nerval.

What are your favourite poems by the Symbolist poets?

Baudelaire's city poems really. The swan poem. The one about old women; the one about the seven cripples appearing out of the fog one after the other – which is pure nightmare. Rimbaud. His 'Petites Amoureuses'. And then a lot of the *Illuminations*. The sonnets too. When he's on the road – sitting about in pubs with his shoes falling apart. The letter 'Reviens, reviens' shows that he did love Verlaine and depended on him, as irritating as he must have been. One reason I like de Nerval is he wrote very little. But he also wrote songs and things for musicals. I like Hugo. When he was eighty-two Judith Gautier got him into bed. A sonnet came out of that. Lautréamont; the scene with the shark and the dead boy, that's my favourite 'book'. Apollinaire too. For a whole winter I translated Apollinaire's *Saltimbanques*. It comes from Picasso really. Where the boy vanishes standing on a ball. And I tried for a whole fucking winter. Every day. And got nowhere.

You carry a line in your head for years... you recite by heart your and others' poetry – sometimes you are finally able to use this line – sometimes, as in the Rimbaud in London prose poem you are not –

As far as my own poems are concerned I can now remember poems I wrote years ago. I think if I were put to it I could recite the Fabliau or Soho poems. This is because I lived with them for so long. There are pages where I am writing the same line over and over. Sometimes a new phrase appears and stays. It's the work of an idiot, the writing itself is idiotic, obsessional. All I can say, which I think to be true, is that all poems begin with words or phrases – and I've got no clear indication when I begin what in fact the finished poem's going to be.

Why do you think prose poetry's so weak in English?

I should say, there's been no history of it at all. In France, before the prose poets – there were people like Rochefoucauld who were writing long aphorisms and maxims, which are the same shape as prose poems although they're not prose poems. There was this long tradition in France of at least this shape of things and I should think it comes from that.

Did you read Philosophy?

In a kind of untutored way. Both Freud and Jung; it was Jung first. Nietzsche. Kierkegaard. Pascal. When it came, the time to read philosophy as philosophy, when I tried to read Wittgenstein it was farcical. I simply couldn't understand it, but in a curious way I realised it was a marvellous way to write poems. Because he writes in such short paragraphs.

What do you realise by night dreams?

I can't remember my dreams. I did remember that one dream, which I put in 'This was the dream'. The extraordinary thing is, in the poem there is the yarrow which grows between the stones. When I remembered the bridge I could very well but it was only in the dream I remembered the yarrow. Which says something about dreams.

Do you think these first four decades have sustained you in Devonshire?

Oh yes ... it wasn't as bad as that in the pub. I quite liked the pub in a sort of way. I liked the language ... it's gone now I think. Some people still talk it. Charlie Weeks [an old friend] talks it. It was beautiful, and funny. They had these curious similes. Weak as a robin. Wild as a hawk. Maized as a wheelbarrow.

When you arrived in West Devonshire what did you think?

I don't know really. And it would be quite wrong to say it was the people I got to know, and the village people, that made me unhappy – because I've known them for so long now and I knew them when they were small children.

Of course, you heard stories in the pub.

Oh very much. You were in the role of father confessor – because they wanted to talk to you and they knew it wouldn't go any further.

Have you a clear memory of the pub after it had closed, the embers in the fire, candles, standing up at the bar willing the pen to write [Seán laughs], exhaustion, despair – a thing of being cursed – not able to write?

I was very unhappy. Not because of the pub so much, but loneliness and a Scottish fallowness. I was missing my own sort. I'd been spoilt. I'd been living with the same group of people since leaving university so it probably didn't do me any harm to be with another kind of people. The candles were real. I hated the generator in the pub – and it didn't like me much and when there was no one staying in the pub I wrote by candle light.

Why have you written so little?

Times when I was trying to write novels: the first years in London. Time spent writing lyrics and sketches for review, then the book for a musical which got lost but the songs exist. Latterly black periods when my poetry seemed a nonsense: all poetry seemed a nonsense.

I only once wrote a poem straight off. 'The nights you walk my love, my sleep.' I wrote another at the same time but discarded it. I'm not ashamed of the small amount of poems. It's not much. The poets I admire, or most of them, didn't write a large number either. I think if I had been able to give up rhyme and stanza forms earlier, not till 'Salathiel', I could have written more. 'Salathiel' was to have been a long poem and my complete break with rhyme. The last part would have been about the great fair at Dumfries. It ended with the drunks in the park. The last lines were: 'Where a drunk man lies on his back / with the moon in his mouth'.

What are your own favourite poems?

Some of the shorter six, eight, liners because they seem to me to derive from Catullus but probably from Landor too. Your poem, 'Where the breached wall'. It is a poem about grief over prolonged, and the last lines are an expression of obssession.

'Salathiel': not perhaps for the poem it is but the one that might have been. It was written with long silences in between. I struggled with it and 'The great gates' together. The last of the rhyming poems and the first of the free verse poems. I had this thing in my head that a poet should write a long poem. But I found it difficult that whole winter when I translated Apollinaire.

I like the poem for Louis because it is a private poem.

You always said you wouldn't want to be buried like Bunting under a mass of speculation; and you'd rather have your work sung in the street by barrow boys.

This is overdoing it a bit ... but the whistling in the street thing is there. I think it comes from Burns, the 'Players', and music hall, where songs first began. Bunting in *Briggflatts* seems to be an entirely different job to early Bunting – there are some beautiful short poems in Bunting.

How long in the Duke of York did you spend on the songs?

It was after the war; I'd started to write before I got to the pub. We did eventually do a review at the 'Players' because I kept nagging, in 1947, in which I wrote half of, at least, and some of it went to another review in the West End. They put on the musical for about sixteen weeks at the 'Players' and I kept writing new songs for it. Lots of people wrote the music for it but I didn't feel any connection with them. Unless I had found someone to sing the songs – because they were really cabaret songs – there's no tradition of cabaret in England at all and there's no singers. There was one girl who could have done it, she was married to a chap who wrote some of the music, and I'd have loved to have written songs for her; but she wasn't allowed to perform because she was French. But there's no tradition like this in England – not like Queneau or all the women Lautrec painted. Jane Avril. Some were English.

It was about the first years at the pub, for one thing we needed money so badly, and I had hopes of this – which was very foolish of me. I should have known better. They did it five years later, but by then the whole thing about musicals changed – and they did a night and a half.

What can you say about continuity and innovation of British poetry from the work you grew up with through to this decade?

I don't really know. Quite honestly. I don't think I'm interested in poetry (that's your lot). I feel more attracted to the people, like Bill Griffiths, that curious – which I didn't know existed – underworld – and that's the wrong word – for poetry. I like the tender care that goes into making his own books. This is marvellous. And he's learning. Bits of Latin, Welsh; and Middle English certainly because *Gawain* is one of the greatest of English poems. No, I like the poems.

Why did you begin writing again in the nineties?

I had time, after Peggie [second wife, d. 1989] died, and you had something to do with it and I had wanted to be free of traditional metres. Bits of 'Salathiel' go back a long way. Three times I've got up to a hundred – I always count the lines; even writing letters, it was writing – sometimes I wrote them as poems, very carefully; wrote and rewrote them.

What do you think of Scotland's attitude to literature in this century?

You can leave me out of this caper – because I wasn't trying to write in a way. I certainly think that MacLean should be honoured for a lot of things – he's done so much to keep the Gaelic language. I knew very little of what'd happened – until I got that Faber anthology and found Tom Leonard, which delighted me. I liked the irreverence. It was at the end of the anthology when things tend to become rather dull and suddenly these squibs started to go off. 'Do you want me to wear something'. But for years I hadn't read it apart from MacDiarmid when I'd been able to read him. He was a Communist and he wasn't one to ingratiate himself in every way – and he fell out with Edwin Muir who must have been difficult to fall out with ... It would have been far better to have a cairn of stones for the old man, instead of that twisted bedstead – but you can't expect much of Langholm.

Are there great city poems in British literature?

No. Not in the sense of Baudelaire's poems. These are beautiful. The ones in *Les Illuminations*, that was already in Baudelaire too. I often wonder what it must have been like to read Blake as a contemporary of Blake's.

What was your feeling when you first read Rimbaud?

Complete astonishment. It means poetry is completely magical and it defeats everybody that a boy of fifteen wrote and stopped writing when he was nineteen.

What are your feelings about Catullus?

Strong. He was a very great poet. The sparrow's track in Louis's poem comes from him. That was one good thing about the pub; I had no money for books so I started to read Latin again, to read Catullus and Ovid, because he tells such marvellous stories.

Villon? Dante?

Villon has a marvellous poem about the helmet maker's wife which is one of the very great poems. I never read the troubadour poets. I've got a wonderful bilingual translation of Dante. 'O tu che vai' is in one of the London poems. I like the canto best about the homosexuals – they're not in hell, though he did put some in hell because they're Florentine homosexuals – but in this one the punishment – though eventually they will go to Paradise – they're made to run through fire; because Dante is still human and opaque he casts a shadow. So one of them comes to him; Arnaut the great poet, and the last three stanzas are all in dialect; Pound and Eliot were always using him.

How did Denis Goacher [who recommended Rafferty's poems to Grosseteste Press] find out that you wrote?

I must have told him. He read my poems once at the Kings Arms in

Winkleigh. An old chap called John Gray took me to hear him. I wore a tie. *Sixteen Poems* is a good selection, apart from this thing about lopping bits off poems which is ridiculous. There aren't really any comic poems are there? There never have been apart from 'Salathiel'...

Have you enjoyed writing?

It's always been very difficult. I've never written an easy poem. Some of them have taken three years. 'Salathiel', a lot longer. But I've got no puff. That rankles a bit, because there was enough material in the root, in the great fair, and tramps have always been there. But I don't remember any great joy, apart from when the poem is finished. And I do think poetry is finished. You know the thing has been done. The trouble is, if you begin when you're seven, the thing is always there. I suppose some people do enjoy writing... I enjoy some writing. I enjoy writing letters. But this last batch has pleased me a lot, because I didn't know they were still there.

How do you feel when you're not writing?

Sometimes I feel rather useless. You do feel as if there is something missing – but then I can't go mumbling poems like Wordsworth. He did.

Have you composed in your head, while walking?

No. I'm very bad about this – I have to see the bloody page in front of me. I'm better now. But I did with some of these last poems. Well, I would – I've got the woodshed now. I used to have the garden seat till it fell down.

You work in the garden every day; there's much less to do in winter, but you still go up. Why did you start gardening?

There was a garden to be gardened at the pub. I worked in the afternoons. And I carried on, up at Nethercott [a farm for city children], after we left the pub. I like vegetables, you can eat them and they don't talk to you.

What's your favourite time of year?

The fall, here. I connect it with children. Capuchin. Louis.

You've often said poetry should be just samizdat, graffiti, or heard as street songs today.

Not all poetry. Poets themselves are a very odd lot and are much nearer to criminals. But everybody's said this in a kind of way. But nobody's believed it.

How have you coped with loneliness?

Writing helped – of course, even if nothing happened, I never stopped. You've got to be tough. Most poets are. You've got to be; they wouldn't exist otherwise. When I suddenly realised what I'd done, moving to Devonshire, I more or less cut myself off from London friends, they thought I was crazed.

Zukofsky, whom you haven't read –

I have read him. He was in the anthology Pound did, where I first read Bunting.

In one of the lines in A *a long poem he wrote all his life he says: 'The melody! The rest is accessory.' Would you agree with that?*

No. I think I always want to have some shred of meaning. It may not be the main one. Not to understand the poem at all is difficult. Mallarmé is difficult for me and to most people I should think.

Is there any great joy you can remember in finishing a certain poem?

I should think the long ones, the London poems, the fabliau; especially the London poems because they went on so – there was so much that needed to be left out of them. They were written here, at the kitchen table, they were both begun at the pub, but I had no hope of finishing them there.

How can you describe your handling of sound?

It simply means saying things over and over again until you get the right sound.

So there's a kind of dogged repetition?

With me there is; because the texts, my manuscripts, look like those of a maniac. I wish I had written some comic poems. Because the review stuff was funny. Comic and erotic.

The lines have an erotic tone. For instance, 'Could it be Agamemnon, was it Troy', that sound, the way the vowels are pushed together is very sensual and masculine. What about the way Sorley MacLean reads, keening away, his lips look as if he is whistling; his whole body is taken over by his sound?

There's not much erotic about my poems. Of course, sound has gone out of poetry hasn't it, rather. MacLean has written quite a lot of love poems hasn't he. I haven't written the love poems I wanted to write. You don't write love poems to people who are dead, do you? And nor are the poems to your daughter love poems. And there's a poem 'Where was that face foreseen, the golden age gone by' which is a kind of love poem, which was written to a real person. And 'To read my hand and find I have no heart' is a love poem. And so is 'When was it first'. What I did learn was, you can make poems out of anything. You can make poems out of Alfie Woodroll, who bored the arse off me for years, bless his heart. Poetry comes from the life you are leading, I suppose.

Do you think that sometimes when you write you don't quite understand the poem you've written – because you've foreseen the emotion that was going to capture you later?

Yes, you do. That poem 'In May the month' was written before Betty [first wife, d. 1945] died. She died so suddenly, which alarms me rather. It wasn't written in its entirety, but it was written...I don't know if grief is the word for what I felt when Betty died. It was a kind of dull rage. Her death seemed so unreasonable. Because Christian was so young she spent most of the war near High Wycombe but at least she had about six months back in Fitzroy Square. She died almost the day peace was declared. I remember Pud [a London friend] made me go out with him on Victory Night. The streets were full with girls with caps that read 'Come and get me' and drunken GIs. 'That they should live and she should die'.

'1945'...

That was one of the poems when I finished, it was a triumph – but there was so much that had to be left out; places and people I suppose, but places, all of them destroyed during the war; restaurants, people.

Why did the accused man refer to St John, Carpenter, Havelock Ellis?

The case was brought against him, because he had two or three cafés, your life was made miserable if you hadn't gone to them. This one was in the Charing Cross Road – it was pathetic – there were one or two transvestites; and they gave him two years for this. 'The curious machine' was a thing he had before he started on this café racket, he carried it on his back. I was once allowed to look inside it, there was nothing in it but coils and coils and coils of wire and a tiny little light like a glow worm and this was supposed to have esoteric powers: and you would see him in streets and on corners of the Charing Cross Road waiting for someone to come and be illuminated.

Did he do this for money?

Yes. You had to pay for it. But how people lived I don't know really. I don't know what Big Ernie did. Little Ernie was a busker. They weren't related. They were all a Holy Trinity. And the other Jack, the mad Jack was a very nice guy indeed; and he lived in a basement flat in Dean Street and he had a row of books which was all Kropotkin and all the anarchists. He was a saint-like character. And he made this terrible drink out of stewed prunes. It was alcoholic in a way I think; but it was made out of prunes.

'Behind the webs of lace curtains the misted windows Time is recording that spring, that year, this place.' I knew that was going to end the poem. Because – in a way, you said I hadn't written many love poems, but these are love poems, to a place.

This poem took a hell of a time...because I'd no idea how the poem was going to go, I didn't know what was going to happen, that the shadow was going to speak – who'd seen 'my shadow acceptable to the shades'. And from then on it was the shadow who was going to speak. And there was the accusation of having left London. Of all the idiotic things I'd done, this was the daftest; because Leonard [Sachs, manager of the Players Theatre] was going to die – so I'd have become a director of the Players, so I'd have been connected

141

with the theatre and I'd have gone on to write for it and I could have made a fair bit of money; and been able to write musicals.

But then you wouldn't have been able to write poems.

This was it, you see. Behind all this, there's always the thing about poetry, guarding this small talent. And of course there was Christian, who needed a mum.

Did you work long hours for the fire service?

You were on duty for forty-eight hours and then twenty-four off. It was exhausting while the city was at war. But you can't believe how exciting it was. Wildly exciting. And all these things, great rattling things came down. You were living through the destruction of a great city. We were in Shoe Lane, off Fleet Street. They simply destroyed Shoe Lane, bit by bit. St Anne's was hit twice. It was burnt out I think, there was only the back wall and this hooped window. Saint Anne is the mother of this poem really. Corbière wrote a whole poem for Saint Anne, for she was the patron saint of sailors. But that's the only poem of his lodged in my mind. He died young; there's only one volume. So did Laforgue. But it's a beautiful poem, and the thing about 'Poor as we are proud' is Corbière too. But then I'd written that other poem for Saint Anne hadn't I.

What do you call the piece beginning 'Histories, histories. Everyone has them' A finale? It's not a coda?

They're two separate poems. There was this break between the work...I didn't know the shadow was going to take over the poem, and that's why his bit is written in italics. And this shadow was the accusing one of having left London. 'Summon the stranger now.' And something did happen, I don't know what it was. I never went back to London again. I went back for two months once – to write a review. It was something that happened and I knew I was finished with London; it had broken the whole thing. One or two people had died.

You are very tender towards the lost people of London, the tramps and the mad.

Yes very much...And the criminals, and the old whores, who were

142

too old to work and wanted to put their feet up and they were mar-
vellous to listen to, the stories: and terribly kind.

'You grow like a beanstalk'.

The house is an echo of Alain-Fournier's *Le Grand Meaulnes*: Hans
Christian Anderson comes into it too. Christian had read *Le Grand
Meaulnes* quite early and was knocked cold by it and probably
incorporated it into her fantasies. I'm glad she comes into 'Thrush'.

'An old man mumbling in a public bar'.

Tick and half tick. They were bores. Some of them weren't. That-
cher was a terrible bore. He used to go on about clocks. My sonnets
were French sonnets. For one thing – it's only got eight beats not
ten; for all the sonnets I read were French; from de Nerval onwards.

'But did I hear or dream'.

I knew Iddesleigh churchyard very well. I must have been an expert.
I used to go and sit in the church during the day and the yard at
night. I did walk there – looking at names. There was a beautiful
yew tree in the churchyard too. That was 'the yew's dry heart'.
Emperor, vagula, nudula, is from a very short four line poem,
supposed to have been written by Emperor Hadrian.

'The great gates fallen'.

I quoted from the minstrelsy; the Grieves and Eliots were inter-
married; the Johnny Armstrangs the first great border thieves – as
a clan from both sides of the border. They go down as far as New-
castle-upon-Tyne. Johnny Armstrang was rescued from Carlisle
castle, which takes a bit of doing. The poem took literally years to
write. It's really about the ballads more than anything else. 'So long
as waters run' is a legal term. The field in the poem was opposite my
house, which I remember my father showing me.

'Not to be, not to be born'.

The line is a chorus in one of the Oedipus plays. I think it must have
been *Oedipus Rex*. It's a very sensible poem. I like this thing, 'the
single bed and rest'. Yeats' version is a direct translation.

'The First Fabliau'?

'Else a great prince in prison lies' is of course Donne. It had stuck
in my mind. It would have stuck in my mind anyhow. I remember
Edwin Muir once saying to me that he found this a mysterious line,
which seemed to me odd. You might say it stuck out a mile what it
was. And I thought one day of a minor prince; and from that small
phrase this began, this poem.

I didn't really know what was going to happen; I didn't know
about the bird really. I'd got 'vesper adest' on my mind because the
Roman marriages were celebrated under the evening stars, and
'Vesper adest' is one of Catullus' beautiful marriage songs, when
he's not being naughty, and my four line poems come from Catul-
lus. Do you know Landor? His four line poems? Beautiful poems.
There's a short poem:

as one stood round, Cairon

a boat conveyed,

less he forget that she is old and

he a shade

Why do you think you wrote four line poems and made it an art?

I think it may be Catullus, because he's got a lot of four liners. And
other people have written four liners. There's a beautiful Robert
Graves four liner, 'Love without hope'. He's odd, Graves.

Did you sometimes reduce long poems to four liners?

There was one long moan and groan which ended with 'epitaphs and
ends'. It's just as well because you can't just write poetry moaning
away. Much better to write erotic requiems which I never did either.
Too late now.

Editorial Notes

SOURCES FOR TEXT

(a) *Poems 1940-1982*
(b) manuscripts
(c) *Salathiel's Song*
(d) *Peacocks. Full Stop*

EDITORIAL EMENDATIONS

(1) 'The night's as dark as a sack': Penultimate line. 'You' for 'your'. Source: b
(2) 'Remembering childhood now': Second stanza, eleventh line, 'God' capitalized
(3) 'Case History': Speech at end of third 'verse'. 'Is there a chiropodist' *?* placed at end of sentence
(4) 'Who has not heard that cry?': Quotation restored from *16 Poems* edition at author's request

STRUCTURE OF *COLLECTED POEMS*

The eight sections from *Poems 1940-1982* were retained by Seán Rafferty in their entirety. The poem order is unchanged, with revisions made from his two errata slips and annotation in *Poems 1940-1982*. The poem '1959' is so titled by the editor, from annotated manuscript.

Between October and November 1993 Seán Rafferty requested that the following poems be added to the book, and these have been placed in the appropriate sections by the editor:
(1) The more the rocketry goes up
(2) Too late, too late, for time to put
(3) Show me a man and I'll raise you the devil
(4) Who would read me 'au soir à la chandelle'
(5) Not to be, not to be born is best

Seán Rafferty wished 'five or six' music hall songs included, but did not specify which titles: Nicholas Johnson and Christian Coupe chose the six songs.

'Rumour of winter in a running wind' is in an unfinished state, a poem Seán Rafferty was trying to resolve for the book. He might not have wished it to be published.

In section IX, as with section VII, Seán Rafferty wished his recent poems to have a section to themselves, specifying his choice for first and last poem. Drawing from sources b, c, and d I have used as closely as possible the ordering structure from c. filtering in four further poems: 'The creaking hinge', 'The long day's dusk revealed', 'He was born', 'The moon has set'. 'The creaking hinge' I presume Seán wished published. 'The long day's dusk' he wished published but not in c or d. 'He was born' was given to editors of c, and d. 'The moon has set' is unfinished; Seán was working on this in November 1993. I have assembled a version from three manuscript variants.

SOURCES DRAWN ON FOR SECTION IX

Salathiel's Song	*Babel*
'Your candles burn. A man walking...'	*Babel*
'The great gates fallen.'	manuscript
'The creaking hinge the falling glass'	manuscript
'The long day's dusk revealed'	manuscript
Leda Poem	manuscript .
Peacocks	*Poetical Histories*
'He was born'	manuscript
'Exegi.'	*Poetical Histories*
'But an old man can summon'	*Babel*
'Remembering childhood now'	*Babel*
'So many come and gone'	*Poetical Histories*
'The moon has set.'	manuscript
'This was the dream'	*Babel*
Thrush	*Babel*

A CONVERSATION

The conversation is spliced together from handwritten replies and oral responses to a questionnaire that became a conversation.